SPLASH OF COLOR

SPLASH OF LIFE

BY

JUANITA RHODENBAUGH

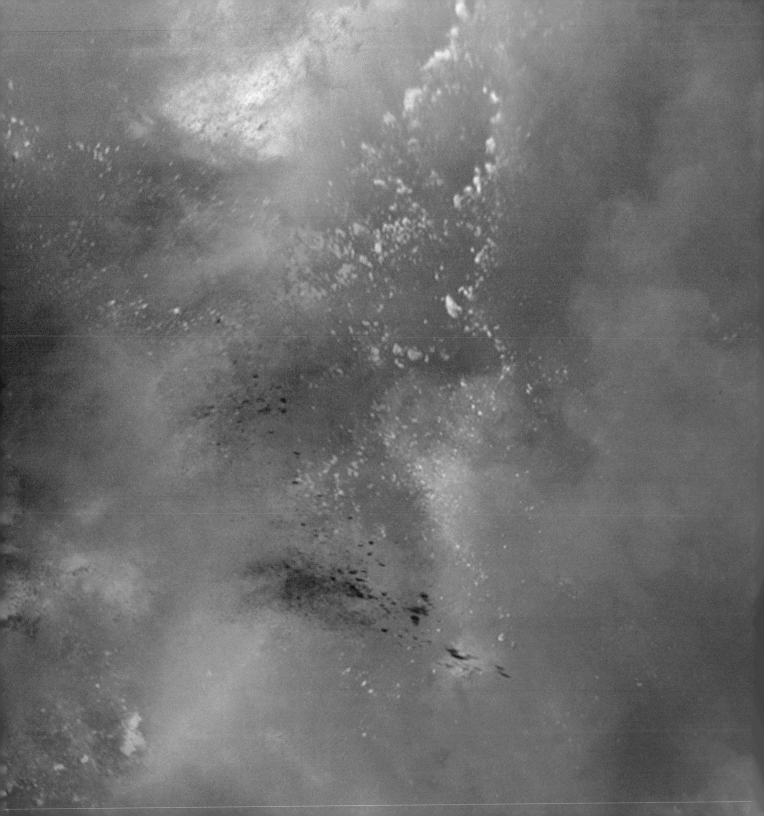

To tell you a little about myself, I am a Polio surviver. Due to the Polio, I suffer from scoliosis and sometimes have to use a cane and wheelchair to get around. Despite this, I am a very active and independent person. From 1983 to 1988 (when my condition was less severe) my family and I spent time in Taiwan, smuggling Bibles into China, and ministering in the Philippines. I have two wonderful children of whom doctors said I would never have. My son, who I lived with for many years, served in the Persian Gulf war. I thank God every day that he made it home safe. My daughter has CP and is developmentally handicapped. She always has a smile on her face and idolizes her brother. Currently, she lives in a group home which she loves as it makes her feel independent. My children and I have been through a lot together over the years. I also have a wonderful grandson who was taught to take good care of his mimi and he does a wonderful job. I truly thank God for the three of them each day.

My goal is to reach out to everyone who has pain. The kind of pain doesn't matter, pain is pain. I am reaching out my hand to as many as I can. I believe this is what the Lord wants me to do, not just for myself but for all those who are suffering.

I know that the Lord is the author and that I am the scribe. What you are reading are pages out of my journals. Come take this journey with me as they are a splash of color and splash of life!

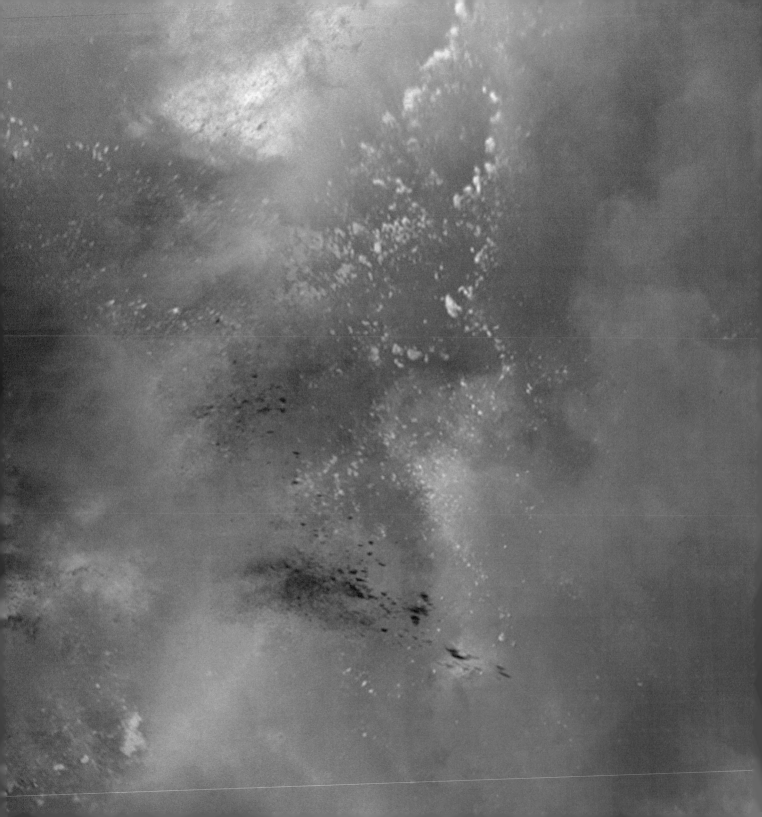

Dedication Page

This is dedicated to my two wonderful children Darrin & Denise, grandson Haden of whom I could have not done this without him and to all of you who continued throughout the years to see this in print!

Needless to say a great love to the real author, God of heaven and earth who allowed me to be His scribe and my hands to form each painting!

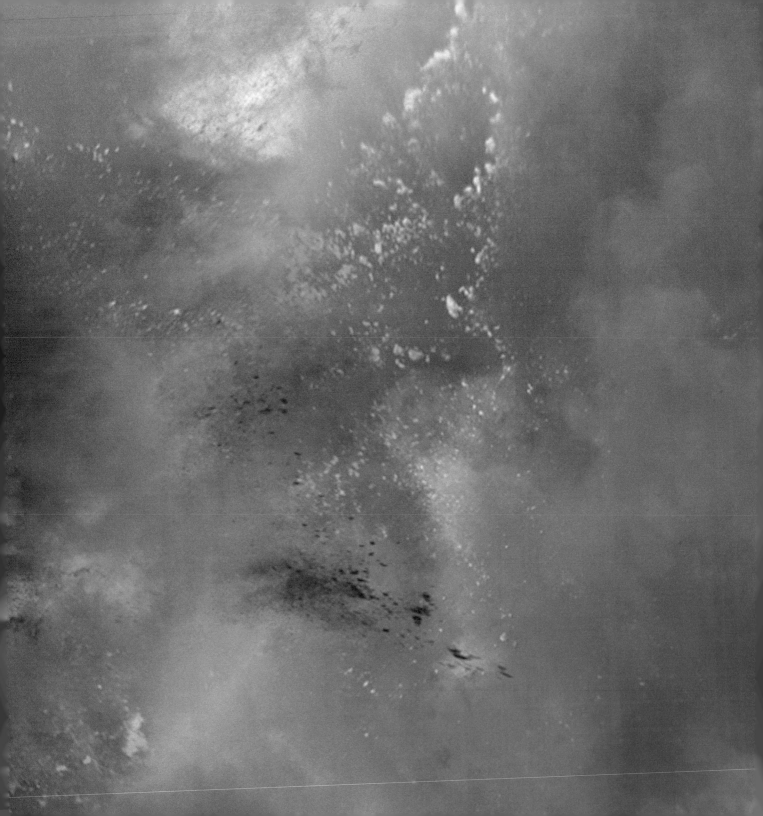

A Child

Have you ever watched a small child that has an ice cream cone?
He has a tight grip on it, but in doing this he tilts it just slightly and
Oop's there goes the ice cream. He stands with an empty cone. He
looks at with tears of dismay. The first thing you want to do is bring comfort to the child. You
wipe away the tears and take him right back to get another one.
I think this must be what the Lord does in the trails of our lives. Sometimes we're holding so
tight, our grip is on the cone but, sometimes it gets tipped and we lose the ice cream. That cone
may be any flavor, courage, faith, hope, or any number of things, missed opportunities
But when it happens the Lord is there to dry the tears and speak
words of comfort. In a sense of speaking the Lord takes you to get
another cone making sure it is filled with what is best for you.
There is not a day, minute, or a second that goes by that He will not
dry our tears or fill our hearts with peace.

A Foot Solider

I am a soldier in your army. I know that I am a foot soldier placed at
the front line of this war. Today I am weary and I'm wondering if just for a
time You could move back a line or two that I might find rest that waits for me.
You know the smile that was on my face yesterday, well today I looked and I can't find it. I know
it's there somewhere in my weariness.
If I could have a minute or two to rest my body and refresh my spirit, how wonderful it would be.
If the front line is where You want me, then that's where I'll be, because I know along the way
there will be times of rest and times to be refreshed.
The smile I'll and wear it with gladness because I know the battle I fight is not for me alone and
I March not alone. Thank You Lord for taking Your place in front sitting the beat to the March.

A Marvelous God

Oh God of heaven and earth
I find out each new day what
A marvel You are!
I marvel that all You had to do
Was speak creation into existence
The heavens and earth,
Every plant, every tree
Yes the grass that grows beneath
Our feet and fish in the sea
Birds in the air.
Oh God of heaven and earth
I find out each new day what
A marvel You are,
Oh God of heaven and earth
I find out each new day what
A marvel You are!
Oh! But when it came to man
Lord, You said, "Let Us make
Man in our image
God You, Jesus, and the Holy Spirit
Worked as one because
You are one!
Oh God of heaven and earth
I find out each new day what
A marvel You are,
Every since You breathed
Life into the creation
Of man The door was opened for

Us to come to You
With Thanksgiving in
Our hearts and enter
Your courts with praise
Oh God of heaven and earth
I find out each new day what
A marvel You are!
In faith believing we can Ask
What so ever we will And
We shall have it
From there we stand firmly
On Your great and strong words,
Knowing You will answer because
Lords it's Your promise
Oh God of heaven and earth
I find out each new day what
A marvel You are!
What a marvelous, fascinating great
Love You have for us,
No matter who or what we are
Your love for us is so
Strong, never waivers
You are there for us forever.
OH God of heaven and earth
I find out each new day what
A marvel You are,
Your love will never leave
Us or forsake us
Your love is so strong that
On matter what is going on
In our lives You have given
us all need from Jesus dying
For you and me
Oh God of heaven and earth

I find out each new day what
A marvel You are!
Great marvelous is my God
His mericies are new every
Morning for you and me
Just reach out, touch Him
And He will sit you free
As He did for me,
It's not the end
Just the beginning!

A Phone Call

I have not been feeling well for some time. On the 25 of July I went to my Doctor and I tell you it was all I could do to make it from the first floor to the fifth which is the floor my Doctor is on. The nurse took one look at me and said you don't look good at all. I told her I don't feel good at all. I was white as a sheet. Blood pressure was really beyond low. The Doctor came in and agreed with both of us. He immediately sent me to x-ray and would not let me leave the office until lab work was done and he got the results. Once all that took place he said I'm sending you over to the hospital. Not in ICU, but what they call 1 step down. Which is on the ICU unit just not in it.

I knew from my Doctor and his nurse reaction that they were really concerned for me. I also knew they were praying for me.

I called my son at work and told him what I knew, he said he would come as soon as he got off work. Which turned out best for me as the nurses and lab people were very busy with me. I knew my life was in real danger, but you know I was so spiritually comfortable and had such peace. I knew what it really meant and felt that peace that passes all understanding was really like. I mean there was no doubt that the Lord God was with me. His presence was so very strong, gentle and it may sound strange but I was full of joy.

I called my friend and said you know I am so comfortable and at peace and rest that whatever happens, if I live or die it was ok. And she said I would go with you if I could. I had four Doctors working to see what was going on. They said they knew I was losing blood, but they didn't know where. The final decision was I wasn't losing it, my body has quit making blood due to several other problems they gave me two pints of blood and I started perking up and strong enough to go home the next day.

I am 70 years old and my Lord and I have been very good friends 50 of those years. I have had many challenges (both good and bad) but I always knew that my Lord would see me through. So if I had I lived or died on July 25th of 2017 that the Lord would see me through.

You see I knew I truly was ready to go home to my Lord or remain and continue being a servant for His glory.

My question to you is simply, are you ready to meet your Savior and Lord when in life or death.

It is His promise once we ask Jesus into our hearts He will never leave us or forsake us. He will always be there for us His beloved children.

A Rough Night

Oh my precious heavenly Father, it isn't just a rough night, but it has been this way for a long time but I trust Your word that promises that You will not put more on us then we can handle and I also know there is nothing new under the sun to You and the fact that you knew me before I was formed in my mother's womb. Although there are times when I find myself leaning on my own understanding Your word tells us not to lean on our own understanding, but in all our ways acknowledge You. Therefore I believe and for many years have believed and know that Your grace will continue to see me through day by day, minute by minute. Thank You for being who You are and for seeing my heart and changing me day by day. I do not fear what may be in my future because I know You are walking with me through it all.

A Thought To Think About

I sometimes say to myself, don't expect the unexpected. Yet I cannot stop from doing just that. Oh yes, I believe in miracles. For me expecting the unexpected is to hope. Without hope we have no faith. My faith is strong, diligent, excited, therefore so is my hope. As I understand you can't have one without the other. One cannot separate those two things. They are a matched set. I put no limit on what I expect continually move forward in faith and hope.

As I said before I believe in miracles, but I also believe it must be in God's time. Maybe I'll never see it in this body of my earthly habitation, but I do know it's waiting for me, somehow, sometime. In the meantime I find that waiting is not lost. There is much we can learn from our inabilities if we allow it to come about. It is ours to choose how we wait.

Don't be afraid to choose. Do not move in fear, but in your God given strength.

Cold Night

It is a cold night, but my spirit is not. I have been to the valley of my mountains. I want to lie down, I want to rest but it seems as though just as I start to rest from doing battle it is time to rise again and do battle, so rise I will.

My spirit is strong though my body is weak. As I draw forth my weapon for battle there is a voice within that calls my name. I know this voice, it is the voice of my love. He knows I know Him and He ask me if I love Him. This is not a question or answer for Him, but for me. My answer is, I love you Lord, I will love You even though they slay me, I will serve you. Then and only then can I breathe in fresh air to renew my spirit, to grasp hold of the hand offered me, to climb the mountain, reach the top, look back and see the mountain is mine, the victory shared between the Lord and I, my rest is complete.

Colors

People often ask why I use to use such vivid, vibrant colors in my art. Simply because they speak so strongly of life When God created the heavens and earth and all of creation He used such vivid, vibrant colors. All you have to do is look around and see this is true. Which tells me the God of all creation is a very lively, loving God to share His beauty with us. To often people spend too much time looking at the blackness of life, instead of seeing the vibrancy of life. In this way we would find bright colors of life when we go through the hard times. Without color I think we would surely wilt. When I'm struggling with my pain I envision bright colors, for they shout of abundance. It gives me strength because these thoughts always bring my thoughts back to the Lord and His goodness to me throughout my life. The biggest blessing is waking to a new day in Christ Jesus. I cannot do my art. I am trusting the Lord that perhaps one day I will be able to do it again. If I can't, I know God the will have other plans for my life, after all it is His to use whenever or wherever He so desires. I gave it to Him a long time ago use however He wishes and I never regretted it for one minute. I could not handle what is taking place in my body without Him!

Come let`s dance
But daddy I`m not able
Yes my child I know

Come dance with me.
But daddy I don't know how.
Yes child I know.

Come dance with me.
But daddy I might step on your toes.
Yes child I know.

Come dance with me.
Lean on me, feel the joy of the step,
The freedom of the dance.

This is really all that God ask of us.

Don't Give Up, Hope Is On Its Way

You know usually the Lord gives me the words to put on paper. But tonight is different as I have no idea what to put down, but I know for sure He will give me the words as I go. I do and have always believed that He is the author and i am the scribe. The following is a letter from God, so read carefully and do not throw it away.

I know the pain you suffer. It was not my intention for any to know pain, and pain does not come from me. Diseases does not come from me.

I can truly say I know exactly what and how you are hurting and suffering. Rather it be from pain of a lost one or pain from spirit, soul, body or mind. You see as in I hung on that cross I suffered all that you and those who have gone before you in every way that was possible.

Because of that I now have the honor of sitting at the right hand of my Father always praying and interceding for all of you.

It would be my greatest desire to see you first to come to the Father through me, and then to say, "hear am I, use me just as I am to be a blessing to all I come contact with. Make me an instrument of joy wherever I go, trusting that in His time I will be completely healed and made we whole.

Love, God

Essence

Yesterday my physical therapist came to my home for the first time. From his questions I realized I must share and trust him with things I worked hard to keep as a personal part of my life. Things I kept as a part of my inner life. Ways of my getting around, I've kept mine because I wanted people to see me Juanita, not my difficulties in getting around. Many know I have polio but, what I wanted and still want is that they see I'm deeper then polio.

Physical therapist ask if I had questions and for the life of me I could really think of one. Simply, how long of a time period are we talking about? Four, six months or a year. I bit my lip to keep from asking. At the same time I realized time was not the essence of this battle. I cannot allow myself to set a time on the goal line but to keep my eyes on faith, hope, and trust in Christ that dwell within. That is essence of my new main climb.

Excitement Of Life

This is a brand new day and with it there is excitement stirring in the air. It's the excitement of life. Each day when I rise I look about me to see what life has to offer and each time I think, there is so very much. Fresh new joy wells up because this is the day that the Lord has made and I will rejoice and be glad in it. It's not what it may bring that factors into this, but that we have the opportunity to take in life for another day.

All winter long every morning at day light I would hear something patter across the rooftop and just before the setting of the sun I could hear it going back over the roof top just chattering away. When spring arrived I no longer heard it, then one morning there it was (a big fat squirrel) running on the electrical wires headed towards the woods. Just as he was ready to jump to the nearest tree he glanced at my patio door, saw me and froze as did I. We watched each other for some time before he went on his merry way

The next morning he was on my porch looking in. I said, good morning and ask him if he knew what wonderful craftsmanship went into him and that God loves all things He created. He waited a few seconds and scurried off to go about his business. He has been there every morning since and we go through the same routine.

It's as if he comes each morning for his own private message. I can't help but wonder how many messages from God we have missed because we were busy with life. And I believe we are meant to be, but with everyday life we let the day go without communing with God and have missed our message from Him. Listen now and He will say, I love you and if you let me I'll handle your everyday life and bring you through the trails of life.

I no longer live in that house but the message is the same. He created all of us and He wants so very much for us to communicate with Him. Sometimes it may be only a word or so but other times He desires for us to fall on our faces and really cry out to Him and if we wait He will speak to us.

This is for all of us, yes for you who are in any kind of pain cry out to Jesus and He will wrap His ever loving arms around you. This is true for all of us. Truly what He wants is for us to reach out to Him for every circumstance. Man's love can waver, His will never, so reach out to Him and hold on tight. He will never leave you or forsake you.

Please don't put this aside, but read it and take it to heart.

Fires

We all have fires to go through, we can smell the smoke, but if we are in an upright relationship with God the smoke or flame cannot harm us. The main thing that stands out in my mind about what Shadrach, Meshach and Abednego did, when thrown in the firey furnace because they refused to bow down to the kings god, but instead they invited God into the fire with. If we invited God into our fires our lives, then our faith, trust and love can only grow deeper. Not only for God but for those around us. It will build compassion for those who choose to go through the fire alone, and to those who invite Him to be in it with them, but do not truly allow Him to join in so they cannot take in what He has to offer them, to go through the fire with victory.

How do we know when we have completely allowed him to join, and not just be there? I think because they didn't allow the situation to control them. Did not allow it to rob them of the peace of God!

Free Spirit

As I wait upon the Lord for healing of my physical body my spiritual body is free. There is nothing that can keep it from soaring wherever the Lord would like to take it. Sometimes my journey walks me into a spiritual truth I had not seen before or perhaps it is a time to talk with Him. Often it is as if I'm beneath a gentle water fall receiving a washing to refresh my spirit. At these times my spirit is very quiet that I might hear the Lord speaking in His language of love. There are times our journey is for pure fun. The Lord comes in my dreams and my body is as free as my spirit. In my dreams often I'm running through a field of daises, or riding a bike down a country lane, or jumping a rope. When I was a child I wanted so much to be a ballerina. Sometimes I'm on stage and I'm doing a ballet with all the grace one could have

I believe this is how God keeps faith and hope living within me. He gives me visual aids. Whatever you may be facing don't give up on your dreams. Dare to ask Him to give you dreams, about the dreams you have in your heart.

I very much believe in miracles. You can trust the Lord with anything you want to say to Him and He truly will hear the cry of your heart.

Through the years I have gained much wisdom. Sometimes the hard way and sometimes not, but what I know is it always matures you in great ways if you let it. If you don't you will go around the mountain again and again. Really just trust Him. He is there 24 hours every day and night. He does not slumber.

Gentle Waters

As I wait upon the Lord for healing of my physical body, my spiritual body is free. There is nothing that can keep it from soaring wherever the Lord would like to take it. Sometimes my journey wakes me into a spiritual truth I had seen before or perhaps it is a time to talk with Him. Often it is as if I'm beneath a gentle water fall receiving a washing to refresh my spirit. At these times my spirit is very quiet so that I might hear the Lord speaking to me in His language of love.

Gliding Up

When I was a child I loved the swings and merry-go-round, I still do.

There was such freedom on these two. On these you could feel the wind on your face, they made feel as if you were flying. Because I couldn't keep my balance I had to sit, so I needed someone to keep it going for me. The swing was different. It's true I needed someone to push me off, but I could keep it going, making it climb higher and higher. It was great exercise and such fun. What wonderful freedom I felt when gliding up, up, up, the challenge to go higher and higher.

This surely must be the way, or it should be in our walk with the Lord. When trails of life come into our lives and we feel ourselves gliding down in our faith and trust, we need to take the challenge and use it to push ourselves higher in our relationship with God. Part of the challenge is to appreciate the gliding down because if you let it, it will help give you the momentum to go higher the next time.

It will give you strength to climb higher in your the Lord. There is not one trail that you go through that the Lord is trying to teach you or someone else. So keep gliding higher and higher, up, up, up, to where He wants you to be.

Glory In This Body

Oh that You might have
Glory in this body.
Oh that You might find
Joy in me Your child.
Oh that You might give
Me one more day.
That when ask,
I might say:
Oh how great Your
Love for me is today,
As was yesterday
And tomorrow will yet be.

God Is So Good

God is good all the time, all the time God is good. Before I knew Him, He gave me a gift, I just didn't know it was from Him. It is the gifts of joy. Many times circumstances have tried to steal it from me but the river that flows into my well goes to a depth that men could not dig. Beyond man›s reach, beyond what the physical body can reach, beyond what the world can touch. Whatever is taking place in my life I can dive into this precious gift. This is not a gift I sit on the shelve but a gift I will always share with others. Gift that will always be mine. All I have to do is draw from the well, and when I do praise will always follow. That is why I can say with confidence that God is good all the time, all the time God is good. Today I share this gift with you, now let us rejoice and be glad in Him. Listen it doesn't matter what your going through draw from the well of living water, the God of heaven and earth is the only way you can get the kind of joy I'm talking about. Don't be afraid to grab hold and hang on tight, don't let go because He won't

God, Mother and Father

Today is Mother's day here in America, but this is a holiday that is celebrated the world around. Not on the same day as we do, but none the less celebrated.

This message is for all parents who lost a child, no matter how many children you may or not have, there is not one of your precious children that can possibly replace the one or ones that has gone before you.

You see I experienced it in my own life. I lost three children. I really thought when I lost the third that I simply could not pick up the pieces. You see because of the Polio they said if I got pregnant again I would lose it also and they really didn't believe that I could even conceive again. I cried out to God He heard my cry, I got pregnant.

I worked at a hospital and one day I began to bleed. My Dr immediately ordered a shot and sent me home for duration of my pregnancy. I told everyone that I was not going to lose this one. About 10 1/2 months later they took him by C-section. My husband kept trying to tell me about him, but all I wanted to know was if he had ten toes and fingers. They said it couldn't happen, but I got pregnant once again and once again I knew I wouldn't lose this one either. She was either early or just a small baby. She has a slight CP. It mostly affected her mind.

But I tell you all this to say, I dearly love both of my living children, but although they help ease the loss of my other children they cannot take their place.

But each pregnancy God was with us, encouraging and supporting us. He promises to never leave us or forsake us.

Before my parents died they buried seven of their children. I can tell you that they loved each of us who remain.

Before my parents died my dad called me every day and one day he said" mama and I cannot bury any more of our children. I believe the Lord heard his cry because it wasn't long before both my parents were gone. They knew Jesus and we are at peace with it.

My advice to all of you who have lost a child one way or another God knows excellently where you are and the pain your heart carries. But I encourage you to let go of your lost ones. I know that my babies are with Jesus and they are safe and happy. If the child that was old enough to receive Jesus but didn't for one reason or another I truly feel so very deeply for you. But the fact remains that the Great God, creator of heaven and earth, doesn't want you to torment yourself any more. Cry out to him and He promises to hear the cry of your heart. Rejoice and again I say rejoice, because His grace is truly sufficient. His mercies are new every morning. He is waiting for you to call upon Him with your pain.

Granted From Above

In You Lord, I have peace, joy, love.
In You Lord, I have strength,
Granted from above.
Though at times my mind and body,
Screams I am weak,
I turn my eyes to You and find the
Strength I seek.
At times I feel I cannot pray but
If I wait on You, the Holy Spirit
Gives me the words to say.
Though at times I get down hearted
And even in despair,
I know it›s ok because, You see,
I know You care.
Though the enemy would try to defeat
And bring me down.
I know because of You, Lord upon
My head You'll place a crown.
I know that as I lay down for rest
And sleep,
You Lord, watch over me because I am
Your sheep
And forever in Your arms I›ll be

Great Period Of Time

This is a great period of time around the world. There are so many who are suffering from many things. Grief, sickness, depression, wounded broken hearts, broken bodies. I'm so glad I serve a God that has promised to take care of these things. He doesn't tell when He will do these things but, that He will.

I think our part is patience to lean in on to the promise knowing that in His time it will come to past. Ours is not an easy one, in fact it's the hardest job anyone can have. No matter where you are in your life, patience is a part of life. Now we may not always operate in it, but the opportunity to do so is given to us every day. If we would make it a gift that we present to those around us we would know joy and others would be affected by it. This is a good thing, so it spread it around. Learn to have joy in your circumstance.

Some of the circumstances in your life may need to be changed. Work at changing them with joy. Call upon the Lord for He has promised to give us a river of living water (John 7: 31, 32), and that He will make His joy in us complete, (John 15: 1-11). These are powerful scriptures. Dare to read them and allow them to be a part of you.

He's Love So Great

Up up and away
Would you fly with me
In the wind!
Up up and away
Jesus came to
Save you and me.
His love so great
He is looking
For the day
When we His
Children will
Reign with Him.
Up up and away
Please come fly
With me in the
Wind.
Up up and away
Jesus came to
Save you and me.

How Does One Know

How does one know when not to fight? If they are not fighting hard enough or perhaps fighting to hard. This I have no answer to. When do you stop looking for answers? Is there a time to stop? I hope not, I pray not.

I think God created me to be strong, seek out answers. I have too many questions floating through my mind not to. The question I never asked is simply, why me. My question perhaps would simply have been, if not for polio would I have been able to help my daughter where others couldn't or would I have been able to teach my son to switch letters and numbers in his mind until it became such a part of him that he no longer gave it a thought? Could I have taught them to be strong and work with their inabilities. And that it's ok because whether we realize it or not we all have inabilities. That one's inabilities can become not only students, but teachers of life. We make decisions to be a positive or negative force. I would hope that I am a positive. Not just for those around me but for myself as well. It seems as though more and more I'm a student and I choose to be. I am forever asking who, what, when, and where of my body. Where once my mind, heart and body were very much one and we were also great friends, no longer seems to exist. Although for sometime now my body no longer wants the friendship I find myself asking who you are. Where once I knew the answers to the questions I no longer know. I long for the friendship but it's as if my body wants to play hide and seek. When I think I have found the answers for the who, what, when, and where, puff, it's gone. This I'm very absolute about, I will not give up on this friendship, it is very precious to me, so I will continue in my quest.. God has entrusted me with this quest. But my greatest quest is not to lose who I am and I will not, as long as I keep myself enfolded in the arms of Jesus, for there is my hope, strength and joy and I will not allow these to be taken from me whatever the future holds for me. So fight I will, I can do no less. For me this is the answer for the beginning of this writing.

Know This

Though you may fly through
Clouds or clear sky;
Though you go through
Waves or clam waters
Of the sea;
Though you go over and around
Mountain tops
Though you may go through channels
Of caves;
Though you may be in the dessert
Hot and dry;
Though your heart may be pounding
With the unknown;

Know This!!
The God who created,
The clouds and clear sky
He is there.
The waves and calm waters!
Of the sea,
He is there
The mountain tops and channels
Of the caves,
He is there.
The desert hot and dry,
He is there.
The heart that is pounding

With the unknown,
He is there.

He is there for you and me,
He is there because He
Knows and cares;
He is there and has called
Forth his His warriors of
Both heaven and earth;
He is there, for you and me,
And we pray in unity,
For calmness of heart,
Steadiness of hands
And peace of mind.

Life Is A Struggle

Life is a struggle for all of us at one time or another. We find ourselves taking three steps forward and wham, before you know it you have fallen two steps back. That's ok as long as we keep our eye on the mountain top and not the valley. Even there, there are rest areas if we look for them. For me, I put pen in hand and create. But it comes in many different ways. Dipping a brush in paint -and create your world of your own. Prayer and meditation is a big to do on my page.

No doubt about now your saying she doesn't know me. I'll give you that, I cannot give you the ability to create, but somewhere within you it's just waiting to be found. It's something you must allow yourself to find, don't be afraid of it. Don't make it a struggle or a war because if you do you will surely loose. Defeat will move in, although you give it only one room, before you know it, it takes up most of the house. But there is still that quiet voice calling "I'll show you where you talent lies."

I remember when I first picked up my brush and began putting my talent to work. It was a 12"by 4"canvas, but it seemed as if it took up most of the room and had me backed into a corner. It was in that corner that I took control and painted my first painting. It wasn't great, but it was the world to me. With each painting my talent improves and brings new challenges. Though I may not be the greatest, it's ok, because it releases something within me.

Whatever you find your talent to be when you move in it, it will help you grow in life. Because God planted your gift in you before you were crated in, your mother's womb.

So even though you may be struggling with something, grab life with great zeal and with a joyful spirit.

May I Help Please

To help someone in pain I think we must understand pain. It doesn't matter what kind of pain we are speaking of. We know pain comes in many forms. Pain is not always a friend, but we should always pay attention to it. If we are not careful how we handle it, it can and will bring self-pity and bitterness, which can paralyze one from moving out of it or at least to find a comfortable way to live with it.

I think fear is a big factor. By not taking hold of the pain it will take control of you. It may be fear of what your letting go of or it may be from what you have already lost. Therefore you're afraid to move forward one foot at a time, because you suddenly realize you may not reach the point you should have.

What I do know is, if you don't continue trying you have no way of knowing if you can reach your goal.

Time is not for you to set, that's Gods. But He can't do His job if you don't let go of the reins. It can be a wonderful time of learning if you allow it to be. Not only for you but for those around you. What I'm asking you to do is to lay the pain in the hands you of Jesus, remembering He will never you leave nor forsake you. He always has His arms wide open.

Some may say, «oh yah, where is He then.» It isn't that He doesn't see you. The plan He has for you is perfect. It is you who doesn't see Him. I urge you to see Him and learn by faith to say, "God I'm yours, I give You permission to use me for Your complete glory," knowing that He may choose to use you just as you are. It's about letting Him use you to bring about the things His word says, to make it very alive to you and those around you. Talk to Him, He will hear you and He will make Himself known to you. You're worth it to Him and the world.

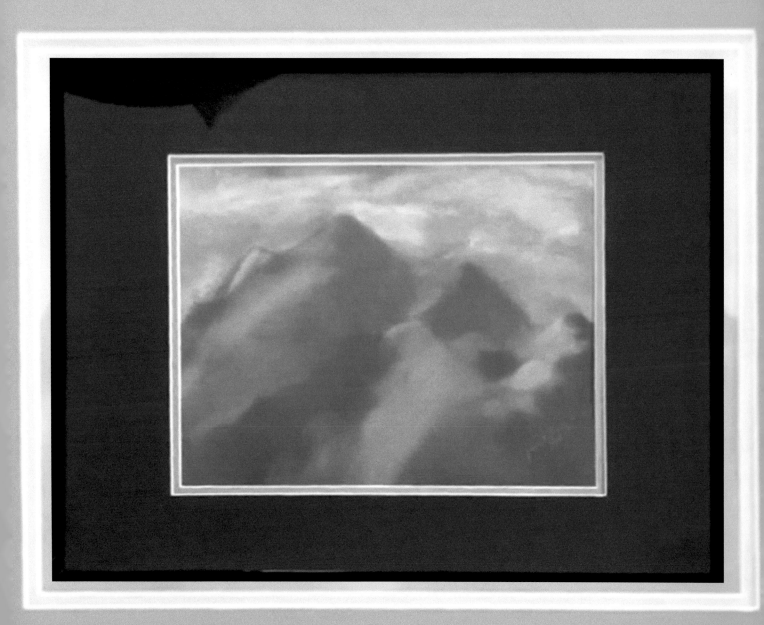

Mountains Of My Mind

I am working on a pastel of mountains. These are not just any mountains, they are the mountains of my mind. When I look at them from a distance it runs through my mind how beautiful they are. But when I begin the climb my perspective starts to change somewhat. The Mountains are still beautiful, but I realize these are not little hills I'm climbing. They are hard, difficult and so very time consuming. There is pain in the climb and it's very exhausting, physically, mentally, and spiritually. At times the pain is so strong that I begin to tire quickly. Other times exhaustion comes slowly.

Which better I cannot say, nor do I wish to weigh one against the other. I only know that in the difficulty and exhaustion of the climb I begin to lose the beauty of the mountains. But there is a voice within me that leads me to draw back to the strength that is within me, which leads me to draw upon the energy of that strength. If I hang in and draw upon that strength to finish the climb and reach the top and look back down the mountain of my life I'll see the beauty of the climb.

This is a day by day climb and yes in my beautiful mountains there are valleys, but there is also an upside of the valley. Perhaps it takes time to see the day by day beauty of the climb and on the climb I see only spots of beauty here and there but more often than not, it's only when I reach the peek and dare to look down do the mountains become alive with beauty. If those around me can see the beauty of my climb I then can hear the voice within saying. "You're running a good race." That for that me is the beauty of my mountains.

In the mountains of my mind I know although I've reached the peek, looking around me, knowing there are surely other mountains to climb and I can see the beauty of the climb.

Maybe your climb is very little compared to mine, and perhaps my climb is little of nothing compared to others. For me that's not the point. The point for me is this, we all have mountains to climb and s really not the climb up that's counts, even though the climb had or has great difficulties, it's after you reach the peak of the mountain, knowing there will be other mountains ahead of you, you have the courage to see the beauty of the climb.

In my introduction I did not tell you that besides the polio I also have severe scoliosis, and my pain level says at about 6 to 7 on a scale of ten and that is with a lot of pain medicine.

My goal is to reach out to those in pain. It doesn't matter what that pain may be and say there is hope.

My Dear Abba

Abba, thank You for past days, present days, days yet to come. Each day You have and do have planned for my life. Yes Abba, there have been times I have messed up and no doubt will again, but Abba, I know it's when I stop leaning upon You, Abba making You known fully again in the depths of my spirit, coming out of the dessert, can I find the path that You are leading me on can I make You known to others to see and know how great Your Love is and where it can take us. It is a journey and it is not always an easy one, but I have learned that through the hard times, the sooner I turn each situation over to You the easier the journey from day to day. Whatever the day may bring Abba God will give you everything you need to get through.

For those of you that doesn't know, Abba is one of the names of God. He has many different names and all of them are for our benefit. I use Abba a lot when I talk with Him, because Abba means daddy and in vision myself curling up in His lap and pour out my heart to Him. That's one reason we should celebrate Christmas.

Abba God sent His son to earth for each of us as a baby, to poor parents and Jesus spent His days in a Manger in a cold barn. Moses was not the first to say, «send me." It was Jesus who was the first to say it. You see the because over two thousand years ago the world was so very deep in trouble by doing all the wrong things that the only way to redeem them was for Jesus Christ to come as I said, a baby, to become a man to minister to all those who were lost in so many different ways. Because the loss was so great,as a man He had to die on the cross for all those who were lost, but not only did He die for them, but for all those from century's to come, that includes you and me.

Now, He took all sin and sickness on Himself on the cross. When He rose from His grave on the third day the first person to see him and reached to touch Him, He stopped them, saying He had not yet been cleansed, that He had to return to His heavenly Father to be cleansed. Jesus Christ took all the filth of the world to heaven where He was cleansed by His Father. He now sits on the right hand of Abba always praying on our behalf.

So you see you cannot celebrate Christmas without celebrating Easter, nor can you celebrate Easter without Christmas. You cannot separate the two.

Merry Christmas to
The world we
Live in

October Air

It is now October, the air has a wonderful fresh crisp feel to it. Someone has wood burning to heat their home. The fragrance of this combined with the October weather is marvelous. It speaks of new things to come. The old is dying, preparing for fresh new life. There is excitement in the air.

We're pulling out warmer clothes. They feel cozy and comfortable. Each day I look for comfort and coziness of the day. For me it is talking and listening to the Lord.

It's as if He wraps a beautiful warm quilt around me and I find myself snuggling down in it to find rest, peace of the day.

With everything that comes into our lives daily to bring upheaval it is important to remember that in the mist of it all the Lord stands ready to wrap us in a quilt of comfort. All we really have to step into it.

Overflowing Gladness

Today, my heart is overflowing. You may ask with what. I cannot tell you why, although I feel as if I'm going to embark on a new journey. I am being given a direction and have no idea where the journey ends nor do I know how.

Yes, I know with certainty that I will meet new people and make new friends. This is exciting as I am a lover of people. More importantly, if we allow ourselves for every journey we take in life, some may not turn out to be what we expected or wanted, the opportunity to grow and gain wisdom in our day by day walk in life. If we find we are lost for directions, we should never hesitate to ask. Yes, men can often give directions and you know in your heart if it's the right path for you. However, the best directions you will ever receive will come from God and His word.

So come friend let's journey through the intricate paths of life, and be stronger for it, for there other journey to take. Oh by the way don't forget there will be stops on this journey. Make the very best of them and there will be rest areas. Enjoy them. Find your treasured rest in the Lord. When you can do these things you have found the purpose of the journey.

Pain Why Must You Stay

Pain, why must you stay?
I open the door, though
It you will not go.
Pain, why must you stay?
I beg you, please go.
Instead you sit pushing deep,
Into the chair of my heart.
The tears, oh no here they
Flow once more.
Surely they will wash you out.
But no, I look in the mirror,
I see you in my eyes.
Pain, why Must you stay?
Yet though I ask you why, I know.
Because death has come to claim
A part of me.
Pain, I no longer ask why
You must stay.
Now I ask you, through
Tears of sorrow,
How long will you stay.
Pain when will you release the heart
So that once again my eyes will
Know the sparkle of life?
When will you move from
My heart, that joy can
Once again flow from me?
Pain, this I know, though the tears

Flow and my heart breaks,
Though I feel as though grief will not leave
The home of my heart,
I say to you, maker of this pain
You may have me now, but
You cannot keep me
I will defeat this pain.
I don't know when, I only know I will.
Because my desire is to live above
And beyond the pain of death.
My faith is strong, my hope keeps seeking,
And when my grief is gone,
The light in my eyes will once again shine
My fountain of joy will once again flow like
A river wide and deep.
My fountain will flow like a water fall,
Powerful, yet calm, peaceful, soothing.
Maker of pain, from my heart to yours,
With love from above, on wings of a Dove.

Passage

Yesterday I read about a cave and it told of all the different passage ways and how easy it is to be lost in the darkness of the passages. I see how this applies to our lives. That these are dark passages in our lives but, if our hearts are turned toward Jesus, He will head us back to the light. What I'm saying is, that in every dark area His to light is there to guide us out of those areas no matter what they may be.

Trials and tribulations are a part of our lives and it's how we go through them that will either make us strong for the next mountain climb and it may not be your mountain. It may be to help someone else climb theirs. This is by no means a new concept. Sometimes we are just too involved in our own mountains and valleys. God bless and keep you until we meet here again next time.

Rain and Sun

The rain is falling.
The birds are tucked
In their homes.
The butterflies have found
Refuge in the trees.
The flowers are drooping
From the rain.
This is today
The sun is shining.
The birds are out
Singing their songs.
The butterflies spreading
Their wings of beauty.
The flowers holding
Their heads high.
This is our tomorrow.
This is me and you,
This is life.

So Deep

The pain is so deep. Tears are deep as well, I think boy if I could just separate from it for a while, look at from afar, could I view it from a different perspective. I came up with yes and no. There is no denying my body tells me that, and you can cry only for so long because it is tears that make the my whole body tense and you find yourself inwardly screaming and sometimes it is in that haze that my body and spirit work together. My spirit can hear a quiet, very soothing voice telling me to breathe slowly, but deeply and the body starts to respond. The tears subside, the body starts to relax.

Still in pain, but can begin to feel gentle hands reaching forth to bring comfort, peace, calmness. Just think of the pain Jesus suffered for you and me. And the thing is, He would do it all again, so when you hear Him call your name reach out and take Him in your heart. There is an old song that says," just call out my name and I'll come running." Well that is all you have to do, just call out His name and He will come running straight to you.

Soar Above

When the heart can soar above the stars or glide as an eagle, if we could, if we would, then when others throw hurts at us, we could glide above and out of the reach of pain, and even dive out of reach. But when we receive pain from another, I think we must soar above the stars of our hurt to fill the pain of others. They truly do not want to hurt alone.

Even though they are blinded to this fact. If you have read or heard this then know why they inflicted the wound, does it really matter to you. Jesus knows.

What you must do is wage war and stand in the gap until you see the fruit of the Spirit in their lives.

Juanita

Son of God

Come and worship Him
Come praise Him
Come lift your voice
Let them ring
Loud and strong

Christ the Son of God
Christ the crucified
Christ the redeemer of all

Come and worship Him
Come and praise Him
Come lift your hands
Up high
Reaching the heavens above.

Spring Is In The Air

As I step outside I can see that spring is in the air. Take in a deep breath, can't you smell it and yes almost taste it. Nature is coming out of its long winters sleep. You can see it blinking its eyes to wake to a new beginning. Right now the waking is slow, but it's there. It has allowed us to take a peek of it here and there. The early flowers are in bloom. There are others saying don't give up I'm on my way. The trees are shedding the last of death to bring forth new life. We too are a part of nature in every way that the rest of nature is. We go through seasons of change. Spring prepares us for the summer soon to come. Summer opens its arms and welcomes us in. Fall prepares us for the winter time. It may be a mild winter and we find ourselves saying, if the rest of winter will stay like this I can handle it. By if the mild turns to be harsh winter we find ourselves praying for spring.

The four Seasons of our lives are unpredictable and often we find ourselves unprepared when they arrive. However there is a way to bring forth spring and summer. We first must realize that fall and winter will surely come our way. They must in order to give birth to spring and summer.

Think of yourselves as a caterpillar in a cocoon waiting for its time to burst forth as a beautiful butterfly. But before the cocoon there had to be preparations made. There is hard work taking place the whole time the caterpillar is preparing to come forth in an array of beauty, that's us! Before we can bring forth beauty we must continually make preparations. How do we do that? We must feed our spirit the right diet. If we do that we will have a warmth within that keeps us warm. The warmth of Jesus will see us through the hardest winter.

So wrap yourselves in the cocoon of Jesus and He will see you through. You will have a beauty that will attract others when you emerge from the cocoon and free of winter for a season. How long will the new season be with us? I don't know, I don't believe we are to know, so we will always stay in preparation for the next season of winter that will bring forth spring.

The Middle

It doesn't matter what time it is when pain and trouble starts it is something that we must take care of sometimes gently or sometimes we with tough voice. Did you know that God likes you to give His word back to Him. For example, Lord your word says, You came to heal the broken heal, sit the captive free, make the lame to walk again and cause the blind to see.

For many years every time I read it I thought He was speaking of the physical body. However the older I got and more mature I have come to believe, that yes He was speaking of the physical, but I also believe our Lord was speaking of the spiritual. I since believe He was speaking of the spiritual as well as the natural. You can't not have one without the other. If we do not grow spiritually.

In order for these things to happen we must know Jesus first. I say that because He says, "you cannot go to the Father without going through Him. Once He is in our hearts, if you trust and obey the words of God you can and should enter His gates with Thanksgiving in our hearts and enter His Courts with praise. Then talk to our Heavenly Father as your best friend.

Make your request made known to Him. In Romans chapter 11 verse 1, it says Faith is the substance (or glue) of things hoped for, but not yet seen.

To me it means to trust in the Lord with ALL your heart and make Him known in All that you do and He will direct your path.

Whatever you need in your life or something for someone you love, you must have faith that it is done because when Jesus died He took it upon Himself. No matter what it is you need, trust Him to know the right time to bring it about.

Begin thanking Him for what He has, is and going to do. You see He really wants to give His people all that they need spiritually and in the natural.

And absolutely remember most of the time He uses people to help with our needs. All things will be done in His time a nd He gives His grace freely.

The Pool

Where is your pain! High, low or in between. You know my pain level this week has been past high but as I encourage myself I'm also sending all who are in some kind of pain to not get down in spirit or discouraged.

Hold your head up high. I tell you to do that because there a verse in the Bible about the pool that an angel would come to stir the water and anyone who got in the water was healed. But there was a cripple man who sit beside the pool for 34 years and he was just wanting and hoping someone would put him in. But no one would put him in. One day Jesus saw him sitting and ask the man why he didn't get in the pool. He told him to take up his bed and walk. What I want to focus on today is the fact that the man sit there 32 before he was healed.

Yes, sometimes healing can take place immediately, but sometimes you may have to wait 32 years or, much longer and maybe not until you reach heaven, if you know Jesus.

But when you fill down call a friend and talk to them. And I would encourage you to put on some music on that will lift your spirit to the heavens, surrendering all your pain to our Heavenly Father or to Abba which means (daddy). Picture yourself sitting in the lap of our great and wonderful God.

Just as God had plans for the man at the pool, He also has great plans for all of us. Tune into Him, talk to Him as a friend, because that's what He is. And Jesus is sitting at the right had of the Father always interceding on our behalf.

If you don't know Jesus I can assure you that there is someone praying for you. So I would say to you, even through your pain rejoice that you have life. Thank

God every day, no matter what may come your way, because God knew you before you were formed in your mother's womb.

No! What is happening in your body God did not do. He is not the only force. There is the devil. Oh i know he is real, as many years ago I seen him and He wanted to destroy me but God sent angels to care for me. And remember angels come in many forms.

So today I challenge you to get to know this wonderful man I have told you about. Fear not for He is wanting, waiting to communicate with you. Whether you know Him or not, He is there for you. Just call out His name Jesus.

I have known Jesus, (son of God, create of heaven and earth,) for 50 years and yes for most of those years God has brought me through some very hellish times, but He has never failed or forsaken me. He is with me always. No I do not always know He is there but when I call on Jesus, God hears the cry of my heart and He answers. Maybe not when or how I would like Him to, but you know it always works out just the way it is supposed to.

So shout to the Lord, all the earth let us sing praises and glory to our King!

The Wonder

I cannot look at nature without seeing my heavenly Father. I stay in awe of it all. But I think the most astounding, amazing part of His creation is that of the human body. I am a people watcher and I ask myself, do they know the wonder of each movement they make and I wonder if they take for granted the precious gift given them. Do they know they are walking miracles? Perhaps I think these things because my own body doesn't make what I assume to be natural movements. It takes no thought, they just move. For me, I must take thought, decide how to move my arms to stay balanced. This has been part of my life since childhood. Yet many times a day I say to myself with humbleness, you are a miracle. Not because of my battle, I might have fought or am or will, but because He created me spirit, soul and body, that is the miracle of life. It is my prayer that everyone, see the miracle that they are, whatever mountain they are climbing remembering it's not the climb but the beauty of the climb.

These Tears

These tears are real. They are mine, and I rejoice in them. They are given to me as a gift. They are my release valve. Tears of pure joy, tears of sadness. Perhaps of confusion, pain (physically and mentally), or of peace, comfort and contentment. You might wonder at my rejoicing in them. I can because I know they were not wasted by simply rolling down my face, but that the hand of God is taking each tear and carefully, lovely, caring for them. They never spill out of His hand. He cleanses each one and warps them in bright wrapping. The tears of sadness become tears of peace and comfort. Tears of pain for tears of strength. Sometimes the gift comes quickly, sometimes we must wait. The package is larger, takes more time for wrapping, but they will always come with ribbons and a note inside and it will always be signed... Thank you for trusting me with your treasures.

Love,
God

United

This Wednesday the 13th. This is not what I usually blog and yet it is very much needed. I grieve for the way our country has become. We are once again a very divided country, a county that was made from the sweat of so many different people and they came in unity to make America not only a beautiful county but one that put God first. God gave us this land not just for its beauty and its challenges. But that we would turn all our pain over to Him.

Well I tell you we have failed greatly in this area. We would rather pick up the nearest weapon, rather a bat, a rock, a gun or whatever else is handy.

Two things, first God chose this country to stand for His people, yes Israel and her people. He says to pray for the peace of Jerusalem. If you by chance read your Bible you will know that this was not a request but a command.

I wonder how we can do this when we refuse to come together as a nation as one united for the people and of the people.

Are we so small minded that we cannot pull together and hold ourselves together for the sake of our government, our children and our grandchildren

We speak one thing to our children and grandchildren, yet we don't live it. Sad to say many children and grandchildren are learning hate towards whoever does not live like we as parents and grandparents think they should.

I'm 70 years old and I can remember when our country went through and still is going through rough, hard times, we would Christian or not, looked to heaven and simply said, "OH God " you may not have realized it but you were praying to the God of heaven and earth,

Let us as a people who cherish the UNITED STATES OF AMERICA. working in unity as ONE. Because that is what God called us to do, remembering that we did not create our wonderful nation. So let us as a great nation, (no matter, race or belief), call upon our mighty and gracious God full of mercy always ready to hear your hearts cry and answer us. Oh let us unite as one, let's us look to the heavens and cry out OH GOD HELP ME AND OUR BLESSED NATION.

Watching For The Dawn

I speak to him and He speaks to me
Hand in hand we face the day whatever it may be
Though with the day may come sadness,
Around the corner there comes gladness,
Even though there may be mourning,
I peek to see gladness has company.
Joy has come to dwell with me!
Though turmoil and trails may come my way,
Peace and calm has come to join my day.
Though pain has come to claim the day,
And with it may come tears
When at night I lay to slumber
With tears upon my cheeks,
I smile to see gladness, joy, peace and calm
Standing strong
As guardian angels standing watching for the dawn.
I know from whom these have come.
I say to Him, " I love you lord."
He says to me, "I love you more."

Weeds In The Flowers

I looked out my patio window at my flower bed to find the weeds were taking ownership of the bed. I began thinking of us, people in the world, as perhaps the way the Lord sees us. We are like a flower bed. All colors and sizes, and His flower beds are full of weeds. Because of the weeds it's hard for the flowers to blend, making a beautiful bed of colors. Like a quilt made with loving hands.

The weeds in our garden can be anything from hatred to simply not making the phone call your heart has been tugging for you to make. We all fit in somewhere. Each day I thank God for His everlasting love and His mercies that are new every morning. I ask Him to show me where and what weeds need to come out. Yes sometimes it's the same old weed that is stubbornly hanging on deeply by the roots, and there are new ones to join them.

God can only make us aware of them if we let Him. He's the one behind the hoe in our garden. In the end our garden will burst forth with beauty. After all it's the beauty of our spirit that He desires.

Weep

Weep my tears weep,
Weep that you may
See the world within.
Weep my tears weep,
Weep that you may
See the world around
You.

Weep my tears weep,
Weep for strength to
Pray love into the
World.

Weep my tears weep,
Weep for compassion
To see the need.

Juanita Rose Rhodenbaugh

Welcomes Me

The bed is strange but it welcomes me or maybe it is I who welcomes it or maybe it is the two of us working together. I curl up in a comfortable position and finding this is no small task. Close my eyes and put my mind at peace. I have drifted off when suddenly me eyes are wide open, for sleep has left me. My body cries out, oh sleep where have you gone, this is no time to play hide and seek. So I call ali, ali auction free. Ah! Sleep has come again. But what! Sleep is gone again. My body cries no, not again. So the night goes on and suddenly you hear a sound, a familiar sound. You find yourself thinking don't be what I think you are. Now comes the decision, turn the alarm off, turn over, go back to sleep or rise up. And when you put your feet on the floor you must decide if you'll face the day with joy and gladness or with sadness. I hope you choose first sitting your thoughts and feelings on things above not on things of the world. Things of the world will come soon enough. But for now, for these few minutes I can think on heavenly things. Though I must face the day the thing I thought of before my feet touched the floor, sit my thoughts aright. Whatever comes my way my first thoughts of the day will be with me throughout the day!

What Is Pain

Pain is many different things to all of us. Take a child for instance, they are playing and they get a scraped arm or knee and you can barely see it, but to them they think they are dying with pain and it's very real to them and as parents we kiss it, clean it up, put a band aid on it and to the child we just became a hero.

But as I have said before there are some pain that you cannot put a band aid on. I speak for myself as well as many of you. My pain is very physical and continues to grow worse and there are many of you in the same boat. Your pain may be emotional, mental, or spiritual physical.

Yes, the cross we carry is very heavy, but I must tell you the cross Jesus carried up the hill for miles and it was so heavy. It weighed Him down and He was so very weak He had to have help. And the pain He suffered on the cross, I tell you ours cannot compare to His. He was not only whipped, but he bore the stripes on His back He was beaten, not just you and me, but for the sins of the world. Not just for that period of time, but for yesterday, today and all the time to come. He now sits at the right hand of the Father always making intermission on our behalf to our heavenly Father for our benefit not His, but ours and generations to come.

Yes many ask how long, when we should be saying use me just as I am. Make me servant, humble and meek. Help me to lift up those who are weak. May the prayer of our hearts always be make me a servant today. In others words, even in the mist of your pain reach beyond yourself to others who are hurting. Maybe not the same way you are but we can relate to their pain. As for me I constantly look to my Heavenly Father to hear the cry of my heart and I know

He hears and He will answer. Perhaps not as we would want but to me I must get my mind off of self and on to being a servant.

I know that some of you do not have that one on one relationship with Him. Well He is just waiting for you to call on Jesus. I tell you it is a life changing experience, you will never be the same again. I so urge you to call on Him. Do not let fear or pain keep you from the greatest thing that can and will happen to you. Make Jesus your hero.

What Will It Take

What will it take
My Lord and my God
For man to make
You Lord of all

When will man see
That You will be
There for them
From here to eternity

Why can man
Not let go
Of the pain of
Spirit, body and soul
That they may grow

Oh what joy they
Would know
If they would see
That You love them
So.

Where

Where did the comfort of my bed go? I cannot find it. It doesn't which way I turn my does not enfold me. But no it's not the bed at all, it's my body that has refused the comfort.

Surely if I can curl up in a ball my body would find comfort however, my body will not allow this. I have found that my pain cries for the fetal position. Back to the womb. Though my body I travel there in my mind. By now you're thinking how strange, however it's not. You see its enclosing myself in comfort that I'm seeking, for me it is thinking on wherever is true. Whatever is pure, whatever is noble, whatever is right, whatever is admirable, if anything is exciting or praiseworthy. I think on these to see me through the tough times. I take comfort in the fact that I'm not alone in this battle. There is that peace that passes all understanding. The Lord is with me through it all. This for me is the warmth of the womb.

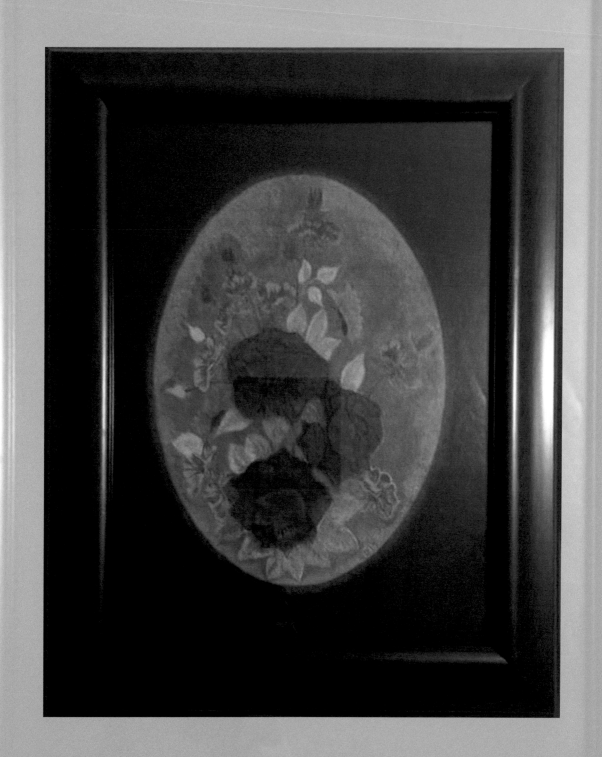

Why

I wonder why there are some who look at a rose and see only the thrones and not the beauty of it. This flower has such a beautiful fragrance and a soft velvet feeling to its touch. It is gentle, quiet, yet powerful in its message. Yes the thrones are there but the beauty of the flower goes much deeper. This how are day to day life is. When trails, (the thrones of life), come to us there is always a powerful message. Let's be sure to search for the complete message of our daily lives, for it will always be there.

Zone Out

<u>Tonight</u> I do not feel strong, in fact I feel very weak. And at this point I'm only asking if it will ever go away. It sometimes is so strong I lose my strength to fight. So I Will Do what I can to pull back from it and zone out. I'm sitting my body aside as much as I can. I'm turning my thoughts to good. I think of my home and see Gods hand at work, next my children, in them I too see God's at work in their lives, though at times they do not see it. But then they are no different than most of us. Oh my friends, how precious. They know I don't like to talk in detail of my pain and they don't need me to. They know to pray. I turn to my art and writing and creating. This brings a turn since of who I am inwardly. I spend time with the Father of heaven and earth. I may not understand the total of why but I always know God has a purpose. I ask what it is that I am to learn today and to whom and to what I am to share. In writing this I know I I know there is a strength restoring me by His love and mercy. Because of this I am able to fight again.

You Are Lord

You Are Lord

You are my today and my tomorrow
You are not my yesterday.

You are my present and my future
You are not my past.

You are mighty
King of kings
Lord of Lords

Great and marvelous
Are You God of all
Creation

I love You Lord
Oh so very much
I love You Lord

Each new day i
Learn more and more
Of who and what You are
How deep Your love goes

I am an open vessel
Fill me continually
Oh Lord how
Very divine You are

Printed in the United States
By Bookmasters